Index

Trading Online...3

   Chapter 1 - Online trading 5

      1.1 - The birth and evolution of trading...10

      1.2 – The requirements to become a trader 33

   Chapter 2 - Online trading tools...................45

      2.1 – The main financial instruments traded 48

      2.2 – Futures 71

      2.3 – The law of trading 92

   Chapter 3 - Online brokers...........................95

      3.1 – The role of online brokers 97

      3.2 – Types of online brokers 100

      3.3 – Supervisory institutions.................105

      3.4 – How to choose the broker to rely on 108

Trading Online

In recent years, financial markets have received more and more individuals. The main reason for this increase is to be found in the mistaken belief that online trading can lead to simple gains, thanks also to the use of platforms that greatly simplify the trader's task.

In reality, the investment activity carried out on the financial markets is not at all simple. Every open transaction and every entry into the market must be the result of a well-designed strategy, but also of an in-depth market analysis. This is because the oscillations present on this type of markets are not the result of chance, but are generated by a series of events: this means that it is possible to anticipate market developments.

It is therefore important for a trader to set certain goals and try to achieve them. The bar will have to rise more and more, but this personal improvement will have to be achieved in a rational way, in such a way as to avoid setting unrealistic goals and impossible to reach.

Chapter 1 - Online trading

Online trading can be considered as the way to make and manage investments in financial markets, from anywhere. It can in fact be done through the use of a simple device with Internet access and a stable and fast connection. It is now possible to manage your investments even from smartphones that, thanks to some apps, allow you to have a view of the market in real time.

Trading online therefore means buying or selling financial products, taking advantage of the low commissions imposed by brokers: the objective is to anticipate future market swings, opening up or down positions compared to the value held by the trend at a given time.

A definition of this kind can make online trading imagine as a simple activity, dictated by randomness, which does not require specific skills. In reality, online trading is a world completely opposite to the one just described. Traders are called to devote time and money in order to study and analyze the market in detail. The objective of each trader is to define a hypothetically valid strategy and to apply it in the market, managing the available capital and the risks associated with investments. This is necessary because every single oscillation object of the trader's study can be seen as the result of the generality of the operations carried out by the subjects active on the market, by the financing bodies and by the stakeholders who have interests on these operations. This means that the oscillations are not the result of chance. Furthermore, price movements tend to repeat themselves in a similar manner over time. Also for this reason the trader is required to analyze the historical series of the single prices of the observed financial instruments, in such a way as to identify affinities in the behavior of the subjects and in the environmental conditions outside the market. Once a match of this kind has been identified, the trader is able to anticipate, with a good chance of success, the future movements of the trade.

So being a trader could be counterproductive. Many subjects have succeeded in making online trading a real job, others a hobby that allows them to supplement their salary, while others have depleted entire assets. The risk inherent in online trading must in fact be managed effectively and incorporated within its own action strategy.

Another essential step in being able to trade online is the choice of the broker. It is therefore necessary to understand the advantages offered by each of them, the guarantee certifications that they hold and the analysis tools that are available to traders. Once the strategy is implemented and the broker chosen as an intermediary with the financial market, then you are ready to invest. Today the main feature of online trading is speed, which allows you to open and close positions in real time. But over the years this has not always been the case.

1.1 - The birth and evolution of trading

The birth of the concept of trading can be traced back to the time of bartering. Trade initially took place between goods of a similar nature, but precious metal materials were soon introduced as exchange elements. This is how the first coins were born, as a guarantee of value and a fundamental part of every exchange, which took on great importance as early as the 7th century BC. With the affirmation of the Roman empire, we are witnessing a considerable increase in the volumes of trade and of the use of money. The population increases, the currency becomes a commonly used asset, especially from the aristocratic part of the people, and purchase and sale operations are carried out continuously.

In the Middle Ages, commercial volumes collapsed and there was a clear financial decline. Specifically, feudalism entailed the closure of monetary and commercial exchanges, which were limited only to guaranteeing the survival of the members of the feud, almost completely interrupting relations with external environments and societies.

The desire to increase the value of its economy to the detriment of the others has led over the years to the creation of new coins, each with different values depending on the weight and the metal used to coin them. Trade thus slowly regained strength and it was possible to witness the birth of a new form of trading. The economy was governed and managed by the powerful, the patrons and illustrious families who ruled the city, and a gradual opening towards external markets, trade between cities and different peoples and the increase in products is witnessed. of the traded goods.

But the birth of modern trading can only be traced back to the historical period in which the banks are born and the creation of the first banknotes occurs. In this way it is possible to transport even large amounts of money more easily, without having to pay for precious materials, even very heavy ones. Both the central bank and private banks, therefore, played a dual role in society: on the one hand they were required to safeguard the assets of individual citizens, on the other hand they were instead charged with the burden of printing and minting banknotes and coins. Initially, especially in the early 1900s, many banks were forced by governments and politicians to print large amounts of money, completely underestimating the risk of entering an even very serious inflationary situation.

Also for this reason it became necessary to create a monetary system able to guarantee a balance both in the press and in the use of individual currencies. The decision to join such a system was taken in 1944, at conferences that later took the name of Bretton Woods agreements.

These agreements identified in the US dollar the currency on which to make absolute reliance, used as a parameter to estimate the actual value of all other currencies. Investors who sought to speculate by using exchange rates saw their chances of success reduced at this time, as the fluctuations reached minimum values and currencies stabilized at standard values.

But the balance achieved with the Bretton Woods agreements took a very short time. In fact the decision to face the Vietnam War forced the US government to print a lot more money, precipitating the value of the dollar and upsetting the financial markets and the world of trading. The various countries in fact decided to exchange the dollars they possessed with gold, an asset considered much safer and less volatile. In this scenario, the President of the United States of America, Richard Nixon, decided to suspend all the decisions taken with the Bretton Woods agreements.

Despite this, the dollar remains today the currency of reference in currency exchanges and financial instruments, although it is not the strongest and safest currency in the world. With the cessation of the effects resulting from the Bretton Woods agreements, every single currency will follow its own swing. The trader is required to identify national and international factors that may affect price trends and their financial trends, in order to identify future developments in the same.

In these years, however, investing in financial markets was not at all simple. Traders, in fact, were required to spend endless hours queuing in front of the banks' branches or in the appropriate venues before being able to open their position, sometimes losing the most profitable time to invest. Furthermore the commissions imposed by the brokers on every single transaction opened on the market were decidedly high, and for this reason trading was considered an activity reserved only for a few subjects, that is only to those who with their capital were able not only to pay commissions, but also to cover the various risks associated with the investment.

1.1.1 – Online trading

The birth of online trading, on the other hand, must be traced solely to the advent of the Internet. The brokers have in fact exploited the possibility offered by the potential of the web, trying to attract as many investors as possible into the world of online trading. To do this, they had to significantly reduce the commission costs associated with each individual transaction, thus also allowing traders with reduced capital to be able to open various positions.

The possible gains, despite the low value of the investment, remain high, thanks to the introduction of so-called financial leverage. Through this mechanism, therefore, the trader can obtain profits of 200, 300 or even 400 times greater than the value of the investment. Naturally the greater the increase offered by the lever and the greater the risk present in the operation that is intended to open.

The brokers, not getting any more profits from the commissions, succeed in obtaining profits exclusively from the spreads, that is from the differences between the levels of the prices of the various currencies or of the various financial instruments. In addition, brokers, reducing commission costs and opening up the financial markets completely, have also enabled inexperienced investors to access the market. This quickly translated into periods characterized by multiple failures, due to the total reliance on the part of the traders. The trading activity carried out without a real capital management strategy has therefore caused a great flow of profits for the brokers: the latter have also been accused of boasting easy profits in order to bring an increasing number of traders to the inside of its platforms.

1.1.2 – The World Wide Web

Online trading, however, becomes possible only after the implementation of a global communication mechanism, which is called the World Wide Web. Thanks to this system, born between the mid-80s and early 90s, computers equipped with an Internet connection could interact, exchanging messages, news and information, even after thousands of kilometers. Also for this reason the web is often exchanged with the Internet itself, but in reality it is a very distinct service that acts through the Internet.

Initially the World Wide Web system (later simply known by the acronym www) was used by physicists and research institutes. Subsequently the universities were involved and, only in 1993, it was decided for the liberalization of the Web.

The potential of this system appeared immediately infinite. The financial markets could not take advantage of the possibilities offered by this scenario, not so much for the attraction of new traders, but above all to guarantee the possibility of opening positions in real time, optimizing the strategies implemented by each individual investor.

The Web as well as allowing the transmission of data, has the function of guaranteeing the security of the financial transactions carried out. In this sense, the evolution of the World Wide Web has taken the road of controlled enlargement. The idea was to follow the principle used in the first Internet communications made for military purposes, so as to be able to guarantee the protection of the data and information exchanged and, subsequently, allow the transmission of virtual monetary values in complete safety.

The euphoria attached to the use of the new means of communication, however, caused a bubble, known as dot-com, which in 2001 caused the failure of a high number of start-ups and websites. The recovery acts as a watershed for all those companies that have been able to survive the IT crack, among which stand the names of Google and Amazon. Even in online trading this bubble caused huge losses among traders, forcing many of them to leave the market permanently. Other subjects, on the other hand, succeeded in wisely anticipating the collapse, obtaining enormous profits and a great success on a planetary level.

The World Wide Web from these years becomes one of the main elements of any market, including the financial one, being used consistently by the subjects both in the workplace and in the personal sphere.

1.1.3 – The American financial revolution

Already from the 1970s until the early 2000s, the United States is experiencing a period that is called a financial revolution. In these thirty years, characterized by a liberalist conception of the market, there is a considerable and constant increase in liquidity, new financial instruments are born that conquer the markets and the prices of goods, especially oil, undergo a considerable rise: the revolution financial becomes thus an almost inevitable consequence of the conditions created in the world.

The financial instruments in this period are characterized by a very high rate of volatility and speculation, with generally short-term flows and with a management by the funds and the appointed bodies that does not show any correlation with the performance of the real economy. All financial companies therefore implement their own strategies in order to obtain profits in the short term, trying to optimize profits: the risk in this kind of management is however very high.

The governments of the various world states themselves are not able to keep up with the speed with which the markets evolve, so they try to remedy this situation by entering into commercial and financial agreements with other states and regions. Soon the volume of world finance exceeds that of global production, thus creating a situation of great planetary difficulty. Banks, companies, businesses and families are therefore driven to debt, encouraged by low interest rates and the possibility of making low-cost investments. In reality these are very high-risk operations, which generally translate into losses: in this way the subjects are not able to repay their debts, sinking into financial failure.

In the United States false positive expectations are created regarding the evolution of real estate markets. Furthermore, the subprime mortgage market, considered one of the riskiest markets, is inflated in volumes and prices through the use of securitization.

The financial bubble that swelled due to all these events, finally broke out in the early years of the new century. In fact the value of the properties grew in such a way as to no longer be able to cover the risks associated with them, and since the securitisations and derivatives used in this sector were real financial instruments, all the financial markets were involved in the bursting of the bubble.

In particular, in 2007 almost all the active subjects had realized the probable financial collapse and decided to invest in so-called safe-haven assets, represented for example by gold, oil or raw materials. In doing so, however, there has been a sudden increase in prices that have driven most of the world population below the poverty line.

Thus we are witnessing a frantic search by the credit institutions of the securities considered as infected. In a climate of total mistrust, however, it appears very complicated to be able to restart the credits, both inside and outside the banking circuits. The consequence is the collapse of the Gross Domestic Product, which can result in a sometimes dizzying drop in production, employment and consumption.

1.2 – The requirements to become a trader

Despite the various tools available to active subjects, becoming a professional trader is not at all easy. In fact some skills are required, some innate other learnable, which each trader must possess.

The first real requirement is the possession of humility. In fact, every trader must recognize what their limits are and act accordingly. To try to respect this virtue it is very important to set goals that are realistic and above all possible. If the trader has already achieved a goal, it is always advisable to close one's position: letting the profits go too far can indeed be counterproductive, and a possible profit could turn into a loss. For this reason it is very important to be able to satisfy oneself, that is to accept what the market offers, without never exaggerating.

The second requirement is commitment. The work required of a trader, in fact, is not simple: he is forced to devote a lot of time to the study of the market and historical series, but also to the implementation of a valid strategy. Commitment and effort are fundamental aspects that an aspiring trader must absolutely consider. That of the trader is therefore a profession that does not allow to obtain easy money, but that, like every other job, requires constancy and responsibility.

Furthermore, each trader must encourage continuous improvement, which can only be achieved through a constant study of the market and with a continuous attempt to broaden their knowledge in the field of stock exchange and finance. This also means that the activity of the trader must be driven by a fundamental passion, which guides every action carried out both during the analysis phase and during the actual investment phase.

Another feature that is required of the trader is patience. On the basis of the implemented strategy, in fact, more or less long periods of inactivity can occur. In particular during the so-called lateral phases of the market, it becomes practically impossible to identify a trend that characterizes the market, therefore it is advisable not to open positions. The trader must not therefore invest following his own feelings and instincts, as it would end up going against his own strategy and perhaps losing part of the capital.

Finally, traders are often asked to compare. In fact, each period of activity can be compared both with the economic performance of the other traders and with their own performance in past periods. Being aware of the effectiveness of the strategy implemented over time is very important in order to remain in the market successfully in the medium to long term.

In addition to these five requirements, there are additional elements that need to be addressed by the trader. First and foremost, Money Management, which perhaps represents the basis of the entire strategy that every investor will have to develop. Secondly, Risk Management, which can be considered a branch of capital management, but which deserves particular attention. Finally, psychology is fundamental, understood as the total abandonment of feelings during each phase of online trading.

1.2.1 – Money Management

Capital management is the main part of an online trading strategy. Traders must indeed rationalize the use of the capital they have available.

Professional traders generally decide not to focus on a single strategy, but to implement multiple plans based on different theoretical concepts, so as to increase the probability of success.

So Money Management focuses its analysis on the decision concerning the amount of capital to be allocated, based on the percentage of risk and the probability of success.

But capital management also means optimizing the investment. The basic rule for a trader is: letting go of profits and cutting losses. Therefore it is necessary that the trader constantly monitors the intensity of a trend in order to understand what is the right moment to open and close a certain position.

1.2.2 – Risk Management

Capital management is opposed to risk management. This aspect of a strategy is very subjective, as it is directly linked to the risk appetite possessed by each individual trader. A high risk appetite allows early opening and postponed closure of certain transactions. It is however essential to establish what is the limit beyond which a trader is no longer willing to take the risk. These limits should never be exceeded, as otherwise we would risk sending the whole strategy to the air, suffering huge losses and giving up important profits.

To limit the risks it is therefore good to establish the levels of supports and resistances for each trend. You can set these points using certain indicators, which allow you to identify the hypothetical future levels of maximum and minimum, both relative and absolute.

1.2.3 – Balance and control of psychology

A third element that every trader must try to limit is human emotions. Online trading, in fact, requires a state of total rationality, which leaves no room for attempts resulting from boredom or despair. In fact, traders will have to face different emotions during the entire period of activity, be it short, medium or long. The investor can be euphoric following a positive period, depressed following a negative period, bored during the lateral phases of the market, or tired during the maximum intensity phase of a trend. Each mood, however, must not affect investment activity and must not lead to opening or closing positions without the conditions studied and hypothesised in one's strategy. Therefore the trader must be able to manage his own psychology, constantly retracing his own balance, in such a way that he never loses rationality.

Chapter 2 - Online trading tools

The assets traded on the financial markets are called financial products. However, there is no definition that can fully identify a financial product. This can be understood as a form of financial investment, behind which there is always the obtaining of a monetary value as a consideration.

Also the Legislative Decree n. 58/1998, known as the Consolidated Law on Finance, does not provide a clear and precise definition of financial product, but focuses more attention on the relationship between financial product and financial instrument.

The latter can therefore be considered as a subset of the former.

One of the greatest difficulties for a trader is to find the correct information relating to the individual financial instruments. Nowadays, different web pages report the evolution of products in real time, but the trader must understand which of these sites reports the data and information received by the market correctly, otherwise it would base the entire analysis on incorrect statistics. There are also newspapers that perform the same service but, of course, the data are not always provided in real time and show stock values and not flows.

By paying a monthly subscription, on the other hand, it is possible to access the web pages of the same newspapers, in such a way as to be able to promptly receive all the correct statistics.

2.1 – The main financial instruments traded

Traders must base their analysis on the study of financial instruments traded in the main markets. The study must focus both on the examination of historical series, and on the economic events that could influence the evolution of instrument prices. It is therefore essential to constantly monitor market trends, identify relevant events for economic purposes and mark them well in advance on a calendar and even study all the financial statements of companies that characterize the market.

Specifically, traders must analyze certain categories of financial instruments, such as shares, bonds, derivatives, contracts for difference, option contracts, Exchange Traded funds and futures.

2.1.1 – Shares

The shares are considered the financial instrument par excellence. They essentially represent shares in a joint stock company. The shares are characterized by risk, as the holder is not certain that the investment made can actually be remunerated. The performance of the shares can be divided into two parts: the first is represented by dividends, that is the part of the profit that the shareholders decide to share; the second is instead represented by the spread, ie the difference in value assumed by the share from the time of purchase to the time of sale.

Thanks to the simplicity that characterizes them, shares are one of the most widely traded financial instruments within financial markets. Naturally the shares subject to exchange are those referable to companies listed on the Stock Exchange. In particular, the so-called free float is important in trading, ie the share of equity capital that the company makes available for trading. The free float represents the part of the corporate capital that belongs to the non-stable shareholders. Traders generally decide to operate on shares related to companies that have a high float, although trading in this kind of financial instruments can be complicated, due to high competition, but also due to the possible financial misconduct that the active subjects of the market put in place.

2.1.2 – The bonds

The bonds are a form of guarantee, and for this reason they are defined as credit instruments. These financial instruments have the function of guaranteeing the repayment of the invested capital at the exact moment in which the same security will expire. Furthermore, the reimbursement is increased by an interest rate, which varies according to the duration of the security.

A trader who intends to invest in these securities must take several factors into consideration. First of all the interest rate, as on the basis of this element the future return of the security will be decided. Secondly, the investor will have to understand the total duration of the obligation and the seniority possessed by the security when it intends to open a specific position. It is also important to assess which is the type of issuer of the security, so as to guess what the risk related to the bond may be. Finally it is necessary to analyze all the macroeconomic data that allow defining what is its economic trend. Before opening an operation of this kind, it is also essential to define the type of bond on which you intend to invest. Depending on the nature, in fact, corporate bonds can be state-owned, that is characterized by high liquidity, which instead have very variable interest rates, and finally governmental ones, which instead group the bonds issued by public and state bodies. Therefore, the nature of the obligation also provides important information that can help the trader in his investment.

2.1.3 – Derivative securities

Derivative securities are a particular form of contract that varies based on the value of the underlying asset, ie the shares, bonds or interest rates to which the contract refers.

Derivative securities probably represent the financial instruments that guarantee greater balance in trading. The trader must therefore try to do hedging: his objective in investments of this kind is to speculate on the change in the price of the derivative security compared to the price of the underlying asset. Precisely because of the greater balance, derivative securities play a role of risk minimization within the trading world. In fact, with the use of this particular form of financial instrument the investor is able to transfer a portion of the risk to the price of the underlying asset. This means that the risk linked to the derivative security is divided between the parties that have entered into this particular contract, and any loss would have a decidedly lower impact than any other trading operation.

2.1.4 – CFDs

Contracts for difference, better known with the acronym CFD, are financial instruments that allow traders to make profits by anticipating the evolution of underlying assets. They therefore represent a form of derivative securities, offering affordability, practicality and speed. The trader must decide whether to open their positions upward or downward, depending on the forecasts made on the trend of the analyzed CFD.

One of the greatest advantages of CFDs is that the trader must not get hold of the security in order to be able to trade, as is the case for shares. This means that investors are also exempt from carrying out all the paperwork that results from the purchase of a stock, eliminating all the costs associated with it. Furthermore, CFDs do not have an expiration date, so the trader can decide to keep his position open for an indefinite period of time, even if he will have to consider the so-called overnight costs, that is to say the additional commissions due to brokers for night trading.

CFDs are therefore financial instruments designed to obtain benefits in the short term, investing in the immediate evolution of trends.

2.1.5 – Options and binary options

Traditional options and binary options are two very different categories of financial instruments. Despite the similar nature, due to the fact that binary options are born on the idea of traditional options, the main differences lie in the concept of simplicity of the securities.

A trader who decides to buy a traditional option must focus his attention and his analysis on the extent of the trend fluctuation, both above and below the trend average. The trader must identify the appropriate time to exercise his option, or decide to let it fall. Conversely, the binary option does not allow the purchase or sale of the asset indicated therein, but this is only the basis for understanding whether the binary option will succeed or fail.

An additional difference between these two financial instruments is duration. In fact, the most important simplification achieved on binary options is that they can last from a few minutes to longer periods that include even a few weeks, having a fixed maturity. Once the traditional option has been purchased, the trader is required to constantly monitor it and make continuous decisions on whether or not to keep the open position.

Finally, binary options require significantly less initial capital than is required by traditional options, and this can be translated as a lower risk rate.

2.1.6 – Exchange Traded Fund

The term Exchange Traded Fund identifies the investment funds that are traded within the stock markets as real shares. The objective of an ETF is to replicate, through completely passive management, its benchmark, ie the index taken as a reference point.

It is possible to imagine the Exchange Traded Fund as a financial instrument halfway between funds and shares, which attempts to incorporate the strengths of both elements internally. In particular, ETFs have a low risk, due to diversification, typical of investment funds, and the transparency and speed typical of the shares.

If a trader decides to buy an Exchange Traded Fund, he can invest in an entire index, with returns similar to those of the reference benchmark, in real time and with actual values. It is therefore an ideal situation for the investor, who only needs to adapt his strategy, in order to obtain profits in the medium-long term.

2.1.7 – Exchange Traded Commodity

ETC securities, also known as Exchange Traded Commodities, are financial instruments issued following an investment made in the commodities market. Like the ETF, the Exchange Traded Commodity also directly replicates the fluctuations suffered by the reference assets.

The ETC allows traders to open certain positions on a single commodity, which was not open to ETF investors. Also in this case the advantages refer to a lower risk, due to diversification.

In this sector it is possible to observe a primary market, which can be accessed only by certain authorized parties, defined intermediaries, and a secondary market, which is instead open to all other investors. It is precisely in this second market that ETCs can be traded, with prices identical to those visible on the primary market. This alignment of values between financial instruments in the primary market and ETC is guaranteed by a series of arbitrages implemented by some intermediaries, with the aim of recreating the same conditions that occur in the primary market in a market accessible to all.

2.1.8 – Exchange Traded Notes

ETNs or Exchange Traded Notes are financial instruments similar to ETFs and ETNs, as they fluctuate according to the evolutions that take place in the primary market of the financial product to which they refer. If Exchange Traded Commodities relate to investments made in the commodity market, Exchange Traded Notes follow the market for currencies, rates and stock and bond indices.

It is therefore an extension of the range of financial instruments on which it is possible to invest even without being authorized intermediaries, which the secondary market offers to traders.

ETNs are also derivative securities that have no maturity and allow trading in the secondary market, in the same way as in the primary market, also reducing the costs and risks associated with the investment.

2.1.9 – Futures

A financial instrument that has become increasingly important in recent years is the future, which deserves a more in-depth analysis.

2.2 – Futures

Futures are financial instruments that are traded within the stock market. Both for the structure and for the features, the futures are incorporated within the category of futures contracts.

The futures are therefore standard contracts and not customizable: for this reason it is possible to exchange this type of financial instruments within the regulatory markets, such as over the counter. The counterparties, therefore, cannot modify the clauses of the contract.

The purpose of the contract is to commit one of the parties to purchase, once the title expires, the established activity, which can be either a financial activity or a commodity. The futures can be extinguished both in the natural mode, which consists in the delivery of the traded asset at the expiry of the contract, or with the early settlement with respect to the maturity, which provides for a clearing operation.

2.2.1 – The birth of futures

The way in which futures are traded has very ancient origins. In fact, the need to negotiate an asset not yet possessed, postponing its delivery to a certain future date, arises within the forums of the Roman Empire. Here, in fact, goods were traded, especially agricultural products, which came from territories far from Rome, which the shopkeepers still did not even possess.

In the medieval period, on the other hand, the function of the markets assumed the characteristics of the current markets. In fact, during the fairs that took place periodically in the various territories, farmers and merchants already agreed on the future price of freshly sown products. Once the agricultural product that was the subject of the exchange was collected, the good was delivered to the buyer and the contract could be defined as concluded.

The first modern future market, on the other hand, was born in 1848. On this date in Chicago the Chicago Board of Trade was inaugurated, a market that began as an exchange center exclusively for wheat, but that over the years has also opened up to trade of other agricultural products.

The future currency market was born in 1972. It is a rather recent period, especially when compared to the one in which the other types of market arose. Subsequently the future markets expanded, also incorporating the trading on interest rates. The index futures market, on the other hand, was born only in 1983.

2.2.2 – The various types of contracts

Futures securities can be divided into three types, depending on the asset being traded.

First of all, there are the so-called currency futures. These are contracts through which the parties undertake to exchange a certain currency for another. The peculiarity is that the exchange will take place on the basis of the price held by the currency on the date on which the contract is stipulated. The traders decide to invest in this type of futures both to reduce the risks associated with the trading activity and to obtain speculative profits.

A second type is called commodity futures. In this case the goods covered by the contract are goods, which must be exchanged at a future date, already set, at the price held by the goods at the time of negotiation. This price is inclusive of some costs that are borne by the seller, such as storage costs and insurance costs.

Finally, the third type is that of stock index futures. However, this type of operation differs from that of the previous ones. In fact, the stock indices are not considered to be tradable goods, therefore the prices will not be agreed between the parties, but will be decided by some competent bodies on the subject and authorized to make this particular passage.

2.2.3 – How futures work

However, in the current financial markets the role played by futures has been turned upside down. In fact, traders use futures as a mere speculative instrument. This means that only a very small part, which is between 2 and 3%, ends with the effective delivery of the agreed goods. The remaining part, therefore, is liquidated before the expiry of the term.

In recent years, the willingness of traders to make these contracts very short has also spread. So futures can also end in a matter of minutes, thus losing the real function for which they arose in ancient times. With attitudes of this kind, the futures market has been changed. In fact, today, one of the major features of this asset is liquidity, created following the high level of speculation present.

In transactions that tend to end naturally, you can see a struggle over prices between sellers and buyers. The former will naturally obtain benefits if the price at the time of delivery is lower than that agreed in the contract, and this spread represents a profit for them; the latter, on the other hand, want the value of the goods purchased to be higher than what was actually paid, so that they can be resold and earned. It is therefore a perennial struggle carried out in order to transfer the risk to the counterparty and obtain advantages from bargaining.

2.2.4 – Futures and CFDs

It is very important not to confuse futures and CFDs. Despite both being derivative financial instruments, in fact, there are some differences that place the two securities on different levels.

The first difference lies in the market in which these two instruments are traded. In fact, futures can be traded and traded only within regulated markets; vice versa Contracts for Difference are traded on secondary and standardized markets, such as those over the counter.

A second difference lies in the price of the two financial instruments. The price of futures, in fact, is certainly transparent, being decided in advance and since there is no possibility of variation. In the markets in which CFDs are exchanged, on the other hand, the price may vary, as sometimes brokers can intervene in the natural relationship between supply and demand and change the value of the financial instrument traded.

The presence of a predetermined expiration date involves the formation of spreads with much wider ranges. This is also due to the nature of the futures, which arise as decisive contracts in the long term, but which, as seen, are increasingly reducing their temporal reach. CFDs, on the other hand, have relatively low spread values and are born as short-term or short-term contracts.

2.2.5 – Futures and Forwards

Novice traders can also confuse futures with forwards. Although both are derivative securities, there are some characteristics that differentiate them.

Both titles operate in a similar way, as they are based on the trading of an asset and on deferred delivery at a certain date. The main difference, however, lies in the risk, as within the futures markets there are some organizations, called Clearing Houses, which guarantee their correct fulfillment. The presence of these institutions leads to a significant reduction in the risk rate in the futures markets. All this does not happen inside the forward markets, within which the trading activity does not appear to be completely covered.

2.2.6 – What are margins for?

Every trader who intends to enter into futures contracts must pay a margin. This element takes the form of a security deposit, to be paid to the Clearing House. This in fact becomes the counterparty with respect to the trader in futures contracts: the conclusion of the contract is therefore subject to the payment of this margin.

The margins can be initial, delivery or variation. The initial margins are calculated in a percentage, decided by the CH, of the nominal value of the contract. The initial margin is repaid on the expiry of the future negotiation.

On the other hand, the delivery margin takes the form of a guarantee against the possibility that the price may vary from the time the negotiations are concluded to the time the goods are delivered. So the aim is to reduce the risk of the transaction.

Finally, the variation margin concerns the daily liquidation of all the losses and of all the profits that each participating trader has made during the day. This margin, unlike the previous ones, can only be paid in cash.

2.2.7 – Regulatory authorities and clearing houses

The futures market is therefore less risky than other types of market. The main reason for this guarantee is to be found in the presence of an authority in charge of monitoring and regulating the market.

The regulatory authority carries out various crucial tasks within the futures markets. The first of these tasks is to define and make public the regulation that each subject must respect within the market. The regulatory authority must also authorize each negotiation and define the terms and clauses for each of them, so as to standardize them. But the tasks of the regulatory authority are not limited to this. In fact it is up to it to supervise the market, verifying the behavior and the activities put in place by the subjects authorized to negotiate, also maintaining a constant market transparency.

The Clearing Houses, also known by the acronym CH, are instead private agencies that are authorized to monitor the operation of the future stock exchange. The Clearing Houses, for each transaction defined on the stock exchange, assume the role of counterparty in the stipulated contract. This step, and therefore the definition of the entire future contract, is subject to the payment of margins.

The CH have the objective to guarantee the good end of the negotiation, adapting the futures prices daily. In addition, the CHs are in charge of disseminating all information relating to the market and of interest to investors. Finally, he assumes the responsibility of ensuring the conclusion of the futures contract, overseeing the correct delivery of the good or assets, once the future has expired.

2.3 – The law of trading

Online trading is an activity subject to continuous regulatory intervention. In Europe the reference legislation is Directive 2004/39 / EC, which aims to protect investors and to create a market based on harmony and integration.

In particular, the legislation aims to guarantee security to all investors during all phases of the investment. Individuals operating within the market must possess certain certifications, which guarantee total compliance with the regulations. Intermediaries must also fulfill certain obligations, such as professionalism and transparency.

Every state, both EU and non-EU, has tried in recent years to implement legislation that follows the same logic. The process of integration and harmonization between the various standards has been carried out in an attempt to create a single legislative source from which to draw. In particular, in Europe the creation of a single financial framework has brought significant advantages for those who intend to buy or sell products. In fact, a financial company can nowadays invest in all European markets without having to set up foreign branches.

The legislation created by the European Union, defined as MIFID, is constantly evolving, both to cover possible gaps and to hold on to all the changes that occur daily in the world of finance. The MIFID, therefore, has undergone important changes in 2014, the year in which the so-called MIFID 2 was approved, and in 2017. In particular, this last change has led to important regulatory changes regarding the regulation of the so-called super-fast trading, ie of all those investments characterized by an almost immediate expiry.

Chapter 3 - Online brokers

Every trader who intends to make profits by trading online must necessarily contact an online broker.

In fact, online brokers are the financial intermediaries that link individual traders to assets. Companies of this kind are born with the advent of the Internet and the birth of online trading. Thanks to online brokers, traders are no longer obliged to physically go to the appropriate locations to open a financial transaction, but they will be able to make their investments from anywhere.

In order to make this possible, online brokers have created platforms. These report in real time the various market swings, which are reproduced on graphs.

Some brokers have created their own platforms, equipped with tools, such as indicators and oscillators, able to provide important information to users, while other brokers use external platforms.

3.1 – The role of online brokers

Online brokers play a primary role within financial markets. The traders, in fact, in order to access, almost directly, to the stock exchange must contact a broker. Each broker must be authorized by the competent body to carry out this kind of service, based on compliance with the relevant regulations and the obligations imposed on them.

Over the years, online brokers have become increasingly important within the world of finance. Today some brokers are considered real market makers, that is companies able to manage and monitor the entire market to which they refer. Deciding to rely on intermediaries able to manage the market saves money and time. In fact, online market maker brokers, acting directly on the market, require both lower fees and less uptime. Vice versa, acting through the so-called ECN brokers, that is intermediaries not directly active on the market, involves an increase in both costs and time. Sometimes the opening of an operation passes through several ECN brokers before reaching a market maker broker: in this case the trader risks losing the optimal time to enter the market, obtaining lower profits or, in the worst cases, losses .

Thanks to their position of relevance, the brokers are contacted by the supervisory and control authorities in the case of misconduct and failure to comply with current legislation.

3.2 – Types of online brokers

Online brokers can be banking or non-bank type companies. Only bank brokers can offer their users services related to banking, such as opening and using current accounts. Non-bank brokers are the so-called investment companies and brokers, EU and non-EU, with registered offices in the European Union.

Bank brokers are monitored by the Bank of Italy, while non-bank brokers are from CONSOB.

3.2.1 – Banks

Banking brokers offer their customers two advantages. The first advantage is represented by the possibility of using banking services even during the course of financial activity; the second advantage, on the other hand, relates to the possibility of accessing the so-called interbank guarantee fund, should the banking institution fail. This fund is able to cover every trader for an amount of 100,000 euros.

There are banks that offer basic online trading services, banks that offer advanced services for investments in the financial market and banks that do not offer any kind of service of this kind. An inexperienced trader can decide to approach the world of online trading by relying on banks with the main services, in order to become familiar with the investment activity and improve. Professional traders, on the other hand, rely on banks specialized in online trading, in possession of the most advanced services, able to support very frequent activities and very large investments.

3.2.2 – Securities Investment Companies (SIC)

In the last few years the number of SIC, that is of Investment Firm, has been significantly reduced, despite the completeness of the service offered to participating traders. In fact, the SICs are able to customize the relationship between trader and broker, offering collaborations that adapt to the type of activity that the trader intends to carry out on the financial market.

The reason why many traders have decided not to rely on SICs anymore is the low amount of insurance coverage, which reaches a maximum of € 20,000 for each customer. In addition, SICs offer traders services that are more limited than those made available by banks, and are less likely to adapt to market developments.

Despite this they remain among the most important intermediaries of online trading.

3.3 – Supervisory institutions

In order to guarantee the collection of the amounts earned through online trading, European and national regulations have established a series of bodies, with the role of supervision and control in the financial markets.

The Bank of Italy has the task of supervising the activity carried out by all banking and non-banking intermediaries, which are registered in the appropriate registers. The Bank of Italy exercises its power by carrying out both remote controls and audits in the legal offices of the individual intermediaries.

The Italian legislation has entrusted CONSOB, ie the National Commission for Companies and the Stock Exchange, with the regulation of investment activities and the protection of public savings. CONSOB also verifies compliance with all the legal obligations of listed companies present on regulated markets, providing in-depth checks in the event that any violations are found.

A primary role is also played by the competition authority of the market, which verifies, sometimes even on the direct notification of those affected by misconduct, the presence of misleading and unfair commercial practices, which can lead to the illicit act. This is an activity supporting the policy pursued by the Bank of Italy and by CONSOB.

In recent years, in order to protect the activity of the trader, a series of associations have arisen. These receive the reports of the subjects operating on the market and act in such a way as to lead to a decisive intervention by the competent bodies. Consumer advocacy associations, as well as the Competition Authority, do not require the support of a lawyer for reporting purposes.

3.4 – How to choose the broker to rely on

It is not easy for a trader to choose which broker best meets his needs. First of all, before opting for an online broker rather than another one, the trader must check if the intermediary to whom he intends to rely is in possession of all the certifications necessary to operate in the financial market.

This step may seem trivial, and in reality many traders, for convenience, decide to interact with foreign brokers. In this case, understanding the qualities and requirements possessed by these bodies is more complicated. However, it is possible to request the help of consumer support associations that can guide the choice of the trader. The risk of not ascertaining the quality of the service offered by your online broker is not to see the profits obtained in the trading activity being remunerated.

Once the brokers considered safe are selected, it is necessary to check the type of service offered. A trader must understand on which assets the broker allows to invest, but also the percentage of return on open transactions, commission costs related to the trading activity carried out and the rate of collection of the amounts earned.

All these aspects vary from broker to broker. Therefore the trader must understand which service is best suited to his needs and choose accordingly.

www.ingramcontent.com/pod-product-compliance
Lightning Source LLC
Chambersburg PA
CBHW070418220526
45466CB00004B/1460